PEMA KARPO

MEDITATION CENTER

CHANT BOOK

Table of Contents

REGULAR SESSION CHANTS

CHANTED SECTIONS IN LARGER TYPE

Table of Contents

ADDITIONAL PRAYERS & CHANTS

CHANTED SECTIONS IN LARGER TYPE

Additional Prayers & Chants

Chanted Sections in Larger Type

His Holiness the XIVth Dalai Lama
- An Aspiration Prayer -

May I become at all times, both now and forever,
A protector for those without protection,
A guide for those who have lost their way,
A ship for those with oceans to cross,
A bridge for those with rivers to cross,
A sanctuary for those in danger,
A lamp for those without light,
A place of refuge for those who lack shelter,
And a servant to all in need.

SHAKYAMUNI BUDDHA

THE VERSES OF PRAYER TO THE EIGHT
NOBLE AUSPICIOUS ONES

If these verses are repeated just once before beginning any kind of activity, whatever is wished for will be accomplished in accordance with one's needs. Keep this in mind while reciting.

Om! In the natural, spontaneously present, perfectly pure phenomenal existence, to all who dwell in the auspicious realms of the ten directions, I pay homage to the Buddhas, Dharma and assemblies of the Noble Sangha, I request that all may be auspicious for myself and all others.

To Drönme Gyalpo, Tsalten, Döndrub, Jampe Gyenpal, Geidrag, Paldampa, Kunla Gongpa, Gyacher Dragpa, Nobel Ones, known for your consideration of all sentient beings. Noble Ones, known for your superior display of enlightened activities that grant mental satisfaction. Merely hearing your names increases all glory and auspiciousness.

Homage to the eight Sugatas!

To the youthful Mañjushri, the glorious Vajrapani, the powerful Avalokiteshvara, the noble protector Maitreya, Sai Nyingpo, Dribpa Namsel, Namkhai Nyingpo, the supreme Noble Samantabhadra, utpala flower, vajra, white lotus, naga-tree, jewel, moon, sword and sun! Holders of the excellent hand emblems of supreme noble good fortune.

Homage to the eight Bodhisattvas!

The supreme jeweled umbrella, the auspicious golden fish, the wishfulfilling vase, the mind-pleasing kamala flower, the conch of fame and glory, the fully endowed endless knot, the eternal victory banner, the all-powerful wheel. You who hold these eight supreme precious signs, offered to the Buddhas of all directions and times, you are the creators of delight, to recall your nature increases all that is noble.

Homage to the eight goddesses of good fortune

Tsangpa Chenpo, Dejung Sedmed-bü, Migtong Den, Gyalpo Yulkhor Srung, Pagkyei-po, Luwang, Mig Mi-zang, and Namthü Sei, holders of the wheel, trident, lance, vajra, vina, sword, stupa and banner of victory, who make auspiciousness and positivity grow in the three realms.

Homage to the eight guardians of the world!

With all obstacles and harmful influences pacified, May the work we are now about to begin, meet with ever-growing fulfillment and success, and bring good fortune, prosperity, happiness and peace.

If this prayer is recited upon awakening, all that is meaningful will be accomplished. If recited before sleep, excellent dreams will be observed. If recited prior to going to another country or place, there will be victory in all directions. If recited before beginning an activity, the desired purpose will increase. If recited regularly one's life expectancy, reputation and endowments will increase. Happiness and prosperity will be fully endowed and one's purpose wish - fulfillingly accomplished. All negativities and obscurations will be cleansed resulting in higher rebirth and ultimate liberation. All these accomplishments are the supreme words of the Conquerors.

Thus, in the year of the Fire Monkey (1896), during the third month under the excellent alignment of the constellations; I, Jampal Gyeipai Dorje (Mipham Rinpoche), found this great wish-fulfilling crystal in the lake of my mind.

May all be auspicious!

Essence of all the buddhas of the three times,
sovereign of oceans of the families and mandalas,
lord of incomparable kindness and compassion,
dharma king of the three realms, we bow our
heads deeply at your stainless feet. With our three
gates, we prostrate and take refuge with great
respect. Please grant your blessings to all sentient
beings, ourselves and others. Accept us with great
love, now and through all our lives.

We can never get enough of seeing your glorious
face: the radiance of your smile, like the pistil of a
lotus, and the splendor of your major and minor
marks, like its brilliant anthers, are amrita for the
eyes of all beings. The petals of your compassion
extend everywhere, pervading the three worlds.
Lord of Sages, White Lotus, protect the lake of
our mind today.

In the lake of Uddiyana, on the tip of a lotus stalk
self-existing, spontaneously present emanation
of the Victorious One, you are endowed with the
good qualities of all the major and minor marks:
Padmakara, protect the lotus lake of our mind.

Complete mandala of compassion and wisdom that sees everything just as it is, friend of the night-blooming kunda flower, moon of intellect, you dispel the dark night of all beings. Your unobscured kayas and wisdoms ornament the sky of dharmadathu: Youthful Mañjushri with your lotus, we continually offer you our best, the crown of our head.

Your smiling face is a ravishing white lotus. Your excellent speech is endowed with a net of a thousand light rays. Bestower of supreme intellect, you dispel the darkness of our heart. Sarasvati, glorious lady of speech, bestow excellent virtue.

Protector Nagarjuna, Aryadeva, Asanga, Vasubandhu, Dignaga, Dharmakirti, Dharma protectors Gunaprabha and Shakyaprabha and other warriors: ornaments and supreme ones of Jambudvipa, protect us.

Samantabhadra, Vajrasattva, Prahevajra, Shri Simha, Padmakara, the twenty five - King and subjects, So, Sur, Nup, Nyak, the one hundred tertöns, and so on: gurus of the kama and terma lineages, we supplicate you.

With the fire mind of a lion's roar, you burned up
all the thickets of falsehood in this world and
attained the glorious and gentle amrita body:
Rongsom Chökyi Sangpo, may you be victorious.

Heart jewel on the neck of Upper White Snow
Mountain, in Pleasure Grove, the source of
good qualities, secret yogin, you accomplished
the essential meaning: Longchen Rabjam, we
supplicate at your feet.

Outwardly you are the son of the victorious
ones, Shantideva, inwardly you are the lord of
siddhas, Shavari, secretly you are the supremely
noble Self-Liberated Suffering in person: Jigme
Chökyi Wangpo, we supplicate you.

Through the blessings of youthful Mañjushri,
awareness-emptiness, the eight treasures of
confidence were released from the expanse of
wisdom and you mastered the ocean of the
dharma treasuries of scripture and realization:
Mipham Mañjughosha, we supplicate you.

You bestow on us the trainings in arts and
sciences, and in the sutras, tantras, shastras,

oral instructions, their commentaries, and so forth and grant the blessings of abhisheka: present and lineage gurus, we supplicate you.

Lord whose good qualities are equal to those of any buddha, but whose kindness is even greater than all the buddhas: root guru, we supplicate at your feet. Turn the minds of beings, ourselves and others, to dharma.

THE TREASURY OF BLESSINGS OF THE
LITURGY OF THE MUNI
ADHISTANI DHIKOSHA MUNI
BODHI BIHARATISMA

Namo Guru Shakyamunaye

As is said in the Samadhirajasutra:
> *When walking, sitting, standing or sleeping, if you
> recall the moon of the Muni, then the Teacher will
> always reside in your presence and you will attain
> vast nirvana.*

It is taught:
> *With a pure form like the color of gold, the lord of the
> world is completely resplendent. If one brings his image
> to mind it is the equipoise of the bodhisattvas.*

*The practice of the yoga of recalling the Lord Muni, our
unequalled teacher, is like this. Do the preliminaries by
taking refuge in the Buddha, giving rise to bodhicitta and
meditating on the four immeasurables.*

In the Buddha, Dharma and Supreme Assembly,
I take refuge until attaining enlightenment.

Through the merit produced by my practice
of meditation and recitation, may all sentient
beings receive benefit and attain the state of
enlightenment.

(recite three times then contemplate)

May all sentient beings possess happiness
and the root of happiness.
May they be free from suffering and the
root of suffering.
May they not be separate from the great
happiness devoid of suffering.
May they dwell in great equanimity free
from attachment and aversion, near and far.

(recite three times then contemplate)

The appearances of all phenomena have no inherent existence.
Keeping the meaning of that in mind:

Ah

Unborn emptiness and the unceasing appearances
of dependent arising are the way of illusory unity.

In front of oneself, amidst oceans of clouds of
offerings in space, on a precious lion throne,
sitting on top of a lotus, sun and moon is the
unequalled teacher, the Lion of the Shakyas.

He is gold in color and is endowed with the major
and minor marks. He is clothed in the three
dharma robes and sits in the vajra posture. His
right hand is beautifully extended in the earth

touching mudra. His left is in the meditation mudra holding a begging bowl filled with amrita.

Blazing with confidence like a mountain of gold, his wisdom light rays emanate pervading the realm of space. His retinue of eight heart sons, sixteen arhats, and oceans of assemblies of noble ones form a complete circle around him.

Merely recalling him, one is completely liberated from the two extremes of samsara and nirvana and is granted glorious supreme bliss.

Visualize him as the great embodiment of the assembly of all refuge.

Visualize the form of the Buddha in that manner. Think that he is actually sitting in your presence, and instantly give rise to bodhichitta. The wisdom form of the Buddha transcends all directions, times, and notions of near and far. Therefore, wherever you visualize, he will abide there with certainty.

From the sutras:
> *If you bring the Buddha to mind, he will reside in your presence. He will always grant you blessings and will completely liberate you from all faults.*

Having visualized the victorious one, one gains inexhaustible merit and the resultant virtue will never go to waste.

Through great compassion, you took birth in the realm of the Degenerate Age of Strife and made five hundred great aspirations. By hearing your name praised like the White Lotus, one does not return. We prostrate to the compassionate Muni.

The virtues and riches that I and others have acquired through body, speech and mind we offer, visualizing clouds of Samantabhadra offerings.

All the evil deeds and downfalls we have accumulated from beginningless time we confess one by one with intense remorse in our hearts.

We rejoice in the virtues of the noble ones and other individuals accumulated in the three times.

Please continuously turn the wheel of the profound and vast dharma in the ten directions.

Your wisdom form is like space abiding without change in the three times, however for the benefit of disciples to show the way of birth and death, please always appear as the emanation of the rupakaya.

We dedicate all the collected virtue that we have gathered in the three times in order to benefit all beings pervading space.

Dharmaraja, may this be pleasing to you and may we attain the state of the victorious dharma lord.

We are living in the dark age and are without protector. With kindness please hold us with superior compassion.

In this realm and time, the multiplicity of appearances of the three precious jewels are the expression of your enlightened activity. Therefore, you are the single, unequalled supreme refuge.

We supplicate you from our hearts with confidence and faith. Please do not forget your former great vow and until we attain enlightenment please hold us joyfully with compassion.

With intense confident faith, visualize clearly and one-pointedly the form of the Muni thinking he is actually present as you recite his names and mantra.

Guru, Teacher, Bhagavat, Tathagatha, Arhat, perfect and complete Buddha, magnificent victorious one, Shakyamuni – I prostrate, offer, and take refuge.

(recite this as many times as you can.)

The way of invocation – the recitation of speech using a few syllables from the Prajñaparamita:

TADYATHA OM MUNE MUNE MAHA MUNAYE SVAHA

(do this a few times and then starting with OM, recite the mantra as many times as you can.)

By the power of recalling the Muni's qualities, clearly visualizing his form, reciting his names and mantra and with a mind of faith:

Imagine that a variety of wisdom light rays emanate profusely from the form of the Muni and clarify all obscurations of oneself and all sentient beings.

Contemplate that the correct qualities of the path of the Mahayana arise and that you reside on the bhumi of non-returning.

Exert yourself in doing this practice as much as you can. During breaks make offerings of mandalas and so forth, recite different types of praises to the Muni. Read the White Lotus of Compassion, the Vast Play, the Variety of Rebirths, the One Hundred and Eight Names of the Tathagata and other sutras of your own choosing as much as you can.

Seal this by dedicating the virtue to unsurpassable enlightenment and by making aspiration.

By this virtue, may I quickly attain the enlightenment of the Buddha. May all beings without exception be established in that state.

In order to be as wise as the warrior Mañjushri and to be just like Samantabhadra, I will follow your examples in all activities. I fully dedicate the entirety of such virtue to all beings.

Generally, in all situations of walking, sleeping, sitting, and so forth you should recall the Muni himself without forgetting. Even at night, visualize that the Muni is actually present and that light rays emanate from his form illuminating all directions just as if it was as clear as day. Within this perception, rest in sleep.

At all times, begin by giving rise to bodhicitta just as the Muni did earlier. Follow the life examples of the Buddhas and bodhisattvas of the three times and do not let your precious bodhisattva vow deteriorate.

Within that, perform the general activities of a bodhisattva and in particular exert yourself as much as you can in the yoga of shamatha and vipashyana. Make this free and well-favored life meaningful.

By merely hearing the name of our teacher, the Muni, stage by stage, one travels the path of great enlightenment and reaches the bhumi of non-returning — this is stated in many sutras.

In regard to the mantra taught earlier it is said:
> *All the Buddhas come from this mantra recitation. By the power of finding this recitation one becomes enlightened like the King of the Shakyas and the supreme bodhisattva Avalokiteshvara. By merely hearing this mantra, one accumulates vast and great merit without difficulty and all karmic obscurations are purified. By practicing this mantra, your accomplishment will be without obstacles.*

This prajñaparamita mantra of few syllables has been taught here in this text and in other teachings of the Buddha. By reciting this mantra only once all the evil deeds accumulated throughout eighty thousand billion kalpas will be purified and there will be other innumerable benefits.

This is the teaching on the authentic essence of the tathagatha Shakyamuni. I will explain in other writings, the manner in which one should give rise to faith and exert oneself in the meditations of shamatha and vipashyana.

Ön Rinpoche Ugyen Tendzin Norbu, the holder of the three trainings, made an auspicious offering of a celestial white scarf and urged me insistently to write this text. I did not forget and recently Ön Rinpoche sent the messenger, Tulku Jigme Padma Dechen with a present of gold and so forth and an auspicious celestial white scarf to quickly accomplish this.

Holding to my promise and in dependence on his request, I obtained unbreakable faith in the supreme teacher. At the end of time, holding the mere title of an expounder of the teachings, I, Mipham Jamyang Gyatso a follower of Shakyamuni, wrote this composition at Puntshog Norbu Ling at the side of the mountain Dza Dorje Phanchug.

This work was completed in the Male Iron Mouse year on the eighth day of the waxing moon of the month of Great Miracles.

Through this may there be unceasing marvelous benefit for the teachings and beings, and in this way, may those who see, hear, recall, or touch this, receive the unequaled blessings of the lord of teachers in their beings.

Mangalam.

The Sutra Of The Recollection
Of The Noble Three Jewels

I prostrate to the omniscient one.

Thus, the Buddha, bhagavat, tathagata, arhat,
samyaksambuddha, the wise and virtuous one, the
sugata, the knower of the world, the charioteer
and tamer of beings, the unsurpassable one,
the teacher of devas and humans, is the buddha
bhagavat.

The tathagata is in accord with all merit, which is
his source. He does not waste the roots of virtue.
He is completely ornamented with all patience.
He is the basis of the treasures of merit. He is
adorned with the excellent minor marks. He
blossoms with the flowers of the major marks.
His activity is fitting and appropriate. The sight
of him brings no disharmony. He brings true joy
to those who long with faith. His knowledge
cannot be overpowered. His strengths cannot be
challenged. He is the teacher of all sentient beings.
He is the father of bodhisattvas. He is the king of
noble ones. He is the guide of those who journey
to the city of nirvana. He possesses immeasurable

wisdom. He possesses inconceivable confidence. His speech is completely pure. His melody is pleasing. One never has enough of seeing him. His form is incomparable. He is not stained by the realm of desire. He is not stained by the realm of form. He is not affected by the formless realm. He is completely liberated from suffering. He is completely and utterly liberated from the skandhas. He does not possess the dhatus. His ayatanas are controlled. He has completely cut the knots. He is completely liberated from extreme torment. He is liberated from craving. He has crossed over the river. He is perfected in all the wisdoms. He abides in the wisdom of the buddha bhagavats, who arise in the past, present, and future. He does not abide in nirvana. He abides in the ultimate perfection. He dwells on the bhumi where he sees all sentient beings. All these are the perfect virtues of the greatness of the buddha bhagavat.

The holy dharma is good at the beginning, good in the middle, and good at the end. Its meaning is excellent. Its words are excellent. It is uncorrupted. It is completely perfect and completely pure. It completely purifies. The

bhagavat teaches the dharma well. It brings
complete vision. It is free from sickness. It is
always timely. It directs one further. Seeing
it fulfills one's purpose. It is known by the
wise through their own insight. The dharma
spoken by the bhagavat teaches taming well. It
is renunciation. It causes one to arrive at perfect
enlightenment. It is without contradiction. It is
all-inclusive. It is trustworthy and puts an end
to the journey.

As for the sangha of the great yana, they enter
completely. They enter insightfully. They enter
straightforwardly. They enter harmoniously.
They are worthy of veneration with joined
palms. They are worthy of receiving prostration.
They are a field of glorious merit. They are
completely capable of receiving all gifts. They
are an object of generosity. They are always a
great object of generosity.

*Translated by the Nålandå Translation Committee, under
the direction of Vidyådhara the Venerable Chögyam Trungpa
Rinpoche.* © *1975, 1980 by the Nålandå Translation
Committee. All rights reserved.*

THE SUTRA OF THE HEART OF
TRANSCENDENT KNOWLEDGE

Thus have I heard. Once the Blessed One was
dwelling in Rajagrha at Vulture Peak mountain,
together with a great gathering of the sangha
of monks and a great gathering of the sangha
of bodhisattvas. At that time the Blessed One
entered the samadhi that expresses the dharma
called profound illumination, and at the same
time noble Avalokitesvara, the bodhisattva
mahasattva, while practicing the profound
prajñaparamita, saw in this way: he saw the
five skandhas to be empty of nature.

Then, through the power of the Buddha,
venerable Sariputra said to noble Avalokitesvara,
the bodhisattva mahasattva, "How should a son
or daughter of noble family train, who wishes to
practice the profound prajñaparamita?"

Addressed in this way, noble Avalokitesvara,
the bodhisattva mahasattva said to venerable
Sariputra, "O, Sariputra, a son or daughter
of noble family who wishes to practice the
profound prajñaparamita, should see in this way:

seeing the five skandhas to be empty of nature.
Form is emptiness; emptiness also is form.
Emptiness is no other than form; form is no
other than emptiness. In the same way, feeling,
perception, formation, and consciousness are
emptiness. Thus, Sariputra, all dharmas are
emptiness. There are no characteristics. There is
no birth and no cessation. There is no impurity
and no purity. There is no decrease and no
increase. Therefore, Sariputra, in emptiness,
there is no form, no feeling, no perception,
no formation, no consciousness; no eye, no ear,
no nose, no tongue, no body, no mind; no
appearance, no sound, no smell, no taste, no
touch, no dharmas; no eye dhatu up to no
mind dhatu, no dhatu of dharmas, no mind
consciousness dhatu; no ignorance, no end of
ignorance up to no old age and death, no end
of old age and death, no suffering, no origin of
suffering, no cessation of suffering, no path, no
wisdom, no attainment, and no nonattainment.
Therefore, Sariputra, since the bodhisattvas
have no attainment, they abide by means of
prajñaparamita. Since there is no obscuration
of mind, there is no fear. They transcend falsity
and attain complete nirvana. All the buddhas of

the three times, by means of prajñaparamita, fully awaken to unsurpassable, true, complete enlightenment. Therefore, the great mantra of prajñaparamita, the mantra of great insight, the unsurpassed mantra, the unequaled mantra, the mantra that calms all suffering, should be known as truth, since there is no deception. The prajñaparamita mantra is said in this way:

OM GATE GATE PARAGATE PARASAMGATE BODHI SVAHA

Thus, Sariputra, the bodhisattva mahasattva should train in the profound prajñaparamita.

Then the Blessed One arose from that samadhi and praised noble Avalokitesvara, the bodhisattva mahasattva, saying, "Good, good, O son of noble family; thus it is, O son of noble family, thus it is. One should practice the profound prajñaparamita just as you have taught and all the tathagatas will rejoice."

When the Blessed One had said this, venerable Sariputra and noble Avalokitesvara, the bodhisattva mahasattva, that whole assembly and the world with its gods, humans, asuras, and gandharvas rejoiced and praised the words of the Blessed One.

Lotsåwa bhikúhu Rinchen De translated this text into Tibetan with the Indian païçita Vimalamitra. It was edited by the great editor—lotsåwas Gelo, Namkha, and others. This Tibetan text was copied from the fresco in Gegye Chemaling at the glorious Samye vihåra. It has been translated into English by the Nålandå Translation Committee, with reference to several Sanskrit editions.

THE MAITRI (FRIENDLINESS) SUTRA

This is what should be done by those who
are skilled in seeking good, having attained
the way of peace:

They should be able, straightforward, and
upright, easy to speak to, gentle, and not proud,

Content and easily supported, with few
obligations and wants, with senses calmed,
prudent, modest, and without greed for
other people's possessions.

They should not do anything base that
the wise would reprove.

May they be at their ease and secure –
may all beings be happy.

Whatever living beings there are, whether
they be weak or strong – omitting none, whether
long, large, average, big or small, seen or unseen,
dwelling near or far, born or to be born – may all
beings be happy.

Let no one deceive another or despise
anyone anywhere. Let none out of anger
or hostility wish suffering upon another.

Just as a mother would protect with her life
her own child, her only child, so one should
cultivate a boundless mind toward all beings
and friendliness toward the entire world.

One should cultivate a boundless mind -
above, below, and across, without obstruction,
hatred, or enmity.

Standing or walking, sitting or lying down,
throughout all one's waking hours, one should
practice this mindfulness; this, they say, is the
supreme state.

Not falling into wrong views, virtuous,
endowed with insight, having overcome
desire for sense pleasures, one will never
again know rebirth.

*Note: Buddha Shakyamuni taught this Metta Sutta, which is
found in the Sutta-Nipata section of the Khuddaka-Nikaya
collection. It was translated from the Pali by the Nalanda
Translation Committee with reference to a number of
previous translations.*

Prayer For The Peoples Of This Earth

At this very moment, for all the peoples
and nations of this earth,

May not even the names of disease,
famine, war, and suffering be heard,

But rather may pure conduct, merit,
wealth, and prosperity increase,

And may supreme good fortune and
well being always arise!

His Holiness Dudjom Rinpoche, Jigdral Yeshe Dorje

Dedication of Merit

By this merit may all attain omniscience.

May it defeat the enemy, wrong doing.

From the stormy waves of birth, old age,
sickness and death,

From the ocean of samsara, may I free all beings.

ADDITIONAL PRAYERS & CHANTS

SEVEN BRANCH PRAYER

I pay homage to noble Manjushri Kumara.

To all the tathagathas without exception, those lions of men and women of the three times who abide in the countless worlds of the ten directions, I prostrate inspired by faith with body, speech and mind.

Through the power of this aspiration prayer for excellent conduct, I manifest in mind all the victorious ones. Bowing down with bodies as countless as atoms in all the realms, I fully prostrate to all the victorious ones.

I imagine on a single atom, buddhas as countless as atoms in the universe, each residing with his son and daughter bodhisattvas. In this way all the realms of the dharmadhatu are filled with victorious ones.

With oceans of inexhaustible exaltation consisting of all the sounds of oceans of various types of melodies, I fully express the qualities of all the victorious ones and praise all the sugatas.

With the finest flowers, the finest garlands,
music, perfumes, supreme parasols, supreme
lamps and the finest incense, I make offering
to all the victorious ones.

With the finest clothing, supreme scents, heaps
of aromatic powders equal in size to Mount
Meru and so on, all displayed in the most
sublime of arrangements, I make offering to the
victorious ones. Supreme victory banners and
supreme pennants, all of these again I offer to
the victorious ones.

Through the power of respectful faith in all
the victorious ones, and through the power of
trusting faith in excellent conduct, I prostrate
and make offerings unsurpassable and vast to
all the victorious ones.

Through the power of passion, aggression and
ignorance, I have performed harmful actions
with body, speech and likewise mind. All these
actions I confess, each and every one.

I rejoice in all merits, those of the victorious
ones and their descendant bodhisattvas of the

ten directions, those of the pratyekabuddhas,
the shravakas requiring practice, and the
arhats who no longer need practice, and
those of all beings.

I request all the protectors, those beacons of the
worlds of the ten directions, who have traveled
the stages of the path of bodhi and have reached
enlightenment free from obscuration, to turn the
wheel of the unsurpassable dharma.

With palms joined, I supplicate all the tathagatas
who are planning to pass into nirvana, to remain
for as many kalpas as there are atoms in the
buddha realms, in order to provide benefit
and happiness to all sentient beings.

Whatever small virtue I have accumulated,
through prostration, offering and confession,
rejoicing, requesting to teach, and supplicating
to remain, I dedicate it entirely for the sake of
enlightenment.

*From The King Of Aspiration Prayers Of The Excellent
Conduct Of The Noble Ones. Translated into English by
Khenpo Gawang Rinoche and Gerry Wiener © April 2012*

Refuge And Arousing Bodhichitta

Requesting the Buddhas and Bodhisattvas

All you buddhas who dwell in the ten directions
All you great bodhisattvas on the ten levels,
All you great teachers, the vajra-holders, turn
Your mind towards me, I pray!

Taking Refuge

Until gaining the essence of bodhi, I take
As my refuge the buddhas, all fully awake,
The Dharma of statements and realization
And all the bodhisattvas of noble aspiration.

(recite three times)

Arousing Bodhichitta

As earth and the other elements, together with
space, eternally provide sustenance in many ways
for the countless sentient beings,

So may I become sustenance in every way for
sentient beings to the limits of space, until all
attained nirvana.

As the sugatas of old gave birth to the bodhichitta and progressively established themselves in the training of a bodhisattva,

So I too, for the benefit of beings, shall give birth to the bodhichitta and progressively train myself in that discipline.

(recite three times to take the vow of arousing bodhichitta)

ENCOURAGEMENT AND REJOICING

At this moment my birth has become fruitful; I have realized my human life.

Today I am born into the family of the buddhas; now I am a child of the buddhas.

This is the supreme amrita which destroys death, the inexhaustible treasure which removes the world's poverty.

It is the supreme medicine which cures the world's sickness, the tree which provides rest for beings weary of wandering on the paths of existence.

It is the universal bridge on which all travelers may pass over the lower realms, the rising moon of mind which dispels the torment of the kleshas.

It is the great sun which puts an end to the obscurity of ignorance, the pure butter which comes of churning the milk of the holy dharma.

For travelers wandering the paths of existence seeking happiness from objects of enjoyment, it is supreme bliss near at hand, the great feast which satisfies sentient beings.

Today, witnessed by all the protectors, I have welcomed the sentient beings and sugatas.

Devas and asuras rejoice!

ASPIRATIONAL PRAYERS

Oh sublime and precious bodhicitta,
May it arise in those in whom it has not arisen;
Where it has arisen, may it never decline,
But go on increasing further and further!
May beings not be separated from bodhicitta,

But always be inclined to enlightened action.
May they be cared for by the buddhas, and
May they abandon harmful action.
May the bodhisattvas' good wishes
For benefitting beings be fulfilled.
What the protectors have intended for them,
May sentient beings receive it.
May all sentient beings be happy.
May all the lower realms be forever empty.
May the aspirations of all the bodhisattvas
Of the various bhumis be fulfilled!

PADMASAMBHAVA
GURU RINPOCHE

Prayer to Guru Rinpoche
to Clear Obstacles on the Path

DU SUM SANGYE GURU RINPOCHE
NGO DRUB KUN DAG DE WA CHEN PO'I SHAB
BAR CHED KUN SEL DUN DUL DRAG PO TSAL
SOL WA DEB SO CHIN GYI LAB TU SOL
CHI NANG SANG WA'I BAR CHED SHI WA DANG
SAM PA LHUN GYI DRUB PAR CHIN GYI LOB

Guru Rinpoche, the embodiment of all the
Buddhas of the three times,

Great Bliss, the lord of all accomplishments,

Wrathful Power, the one who dispels all
hindrances and subdues negativity,

Grant your blessings, we pray!

Please remove all outer, inner, and secret
obstacles.

May all our aspirations be fulfilled.

AVALOKITESHVARA

THE MEDITATION AND RECITATION OF THE SIX SYLLABLE AVALOKITESHVARA

For those who wish to practice in a non elaborate manner, first take refuge, give rise to bodhicitta and meditate on the four immeasurables.

In the Buddha, dharma and supreme assembly,
I take refuge until attaining enlightenment.
Through the merit produced by my practice
of meditation and recitation,
May all sentient beings receive benefit and
attain the state of enlightenment.

(recite three times)

May all sentient beings possess happiness
and the root of happiness.
May they be free from suffering and the
root of suffering.
May they not be separate from the great
happiness devoid of suffering.
May they dwell in great equanimity free
from attachment and aversion, near and far.

(recite three times)

After that:

HRIH

In the center of the pure realm of Potala, on top
of a purely white lotus and moon seat, I arise in
the form of noble Avalokiteshvara.

He is luminous white in color and has one face,
four arms and two legs. His first pair of hands
are joined in anjali at his heart. His lower pair
hold a crystal mala and a white lotus. He is
adorned with silks and jewels and sits in the vajra
posture. Amitabha crowns the top of his head.
Surrounding him like thick clouds are Buddhas
and Bodhisattvas.

At his three centers, from OM, AH and HUM,
rays of light emanate. They invite hosts of
jnanasattvas who inseparably dissolve into him.

In the center of his heart, on top of a lotus and
moon seat, is the syllable HRIH. Surrounding it
is a garland of mantra syllables. As it turns, light
rays emanate making offering to the noble ones

OM   AH   HUM   HRIH

and purifying the obscurations of all beings.
All realms are the pure realm of the Potala
mountain. All appearances are the body of great
compassion. All sounds are the speech of the six
syllable mantra. All recollections and thoughts
are the mind of emptiness and compassion.

Within the innate nature of all-pervasive
non-attachment, perform the recitation.

OM MANI PADME HUM

*Thus recite the six syllable mantra or add the seventh syllable
HRIH, whatever you like.*

Then:
HRIH
Look at your mind with mind. Since it cannot
be identified, it is like space. Not seeing anything
whatsoever, it is crystal clarity. Its essential
nature abides in emptiness.

OM MANI PADME HUM HRIH

From within the nature of unobstructed
emptiness appearances are unceasing, vivid and
sharp. They are without partiality, all-pervasive

and unconditioned. This luminous nature —
what a great wonder.

OM MANI PADME HUM HRIH

While luminous it is empty and while empty it is
luminous. The inseparability of luminosity and
emptiness is free from thought and expression.
This is the great bliss of the connate nature. It is
the ultimate definitive Lord Avalokiteshvara.

OM MANI PADME HUM HRIH

*While reciting, contemplate the meaning. In the end dedicate the
virtue and recite auspicious verses.*

By this virtue, may I quickly attain the
enlightenment of Avalokiteshvara. May all beings
without exception be established in that state.
In order to be as wise as the warrior Mañjushri
and to be just like Samantabhadra, I will follow
your examples in all activities. I fully dedicate the
entirety of such virtue to all beings.

*This practice without elaboration whose meaning is in accord with
the tantras, scriptures and instructions was written by Mipham.
Virtue. Mangalam. Translation © 2008, Khenpo Gawang
Rinpoche and Gerry Wiener*

Short Medicine Buddha Practice
(Sangye Menla)

Bhagavat, Tathagatha, Arhat, perfect and complete Medicine Buddha, king of lapis lazuli light, I offer prostrations.

(recite 3 times)

HUM Your body's color is like a mountain of lapis lazuli, you dispel the suffering of disease for all sentient beings.

Surrounded by your retinue of eight bodhisattvas, I praise and pay homage to the Buddha who holds the precious medicine.

TAYATA OM BEKENDZE BEKENDZE MAHA BEKENDZE RADZA SAMUDGATE SOHA

(recite the mantra as much as your can)

May all the sentient beings who are ill quickly be freed from sickness and may all the illnesses of beings never arise again.

Tibetan pronounciation:
Tah-yah-tah OM, beck-and-zay beck-and-zay, mah-hah beck-and-zay, rod-zah sah-moo-gah-tay, so-hah!

Prayer to Arya Tara

OM

I pay homage to the Venerable TARE Goddess.

The one called TUTTARE who protects from all torment.

The heroine TURE of unobstructed compassion.

Please grant me supreme accomplishment.

SVAHA

OM TARE TUTTARE TURE SVAHA

(recite the mantra as much as your can)

May There Be Virtue.
Prayer written by Ju Mipham
Translated by Khenpo Gawang Rinpoche and Gerry Wiener

PRAISE TO MANJUSHRI

Homage to the Bhagavan, the Lord Protector
Manjushri

Your wisdom, free from the cloud of the two
obscurations, is pure and brilliant like the sun.

To symbolize knowing the meaning of all
phenomena just as it is, you hold a scripture
at your heart.

You love, like an only child, all sentient beings
caught in the prison of samsara; overwhelmed
with suffering and the thick darkness of
ignorance.

Thundering like a dragon, with the speech of
sixty melodious tones, your voice awakens
beings from the slumber of delusions, and frees
them from the chains of karma.

You hold a sword aloft to cut every shoot of
suffering and dispel the darkness of ignorance.

Pure from the beginning, you have reached the

pinnacle of the ten stages and perfected all noble qualities.

Foremost among the children of the victorious ones, your form is adorned with the hundred and twelve ornaments.

To Manjushri, the dispeller of ignorance in my mind, I pay homage.

OM A RA PA TSA NA DHI

(recite the mantra as much as your can)

Oh! Loving one, may the rays of your supreme wisdom completely dispel my mind's gloom of ignorance.

Please give me confidence and wisdom so I may realize the meaning of the texts of the Buddha's teachings and commentaries.

Translated by Khenpo Gawang Rinpoche and Candia Ludy May, 2013

YESHE TSOGYAL

THE LONGING MELODY OF FAITH

E MA HO! Wondrous!
Vajrayogini, mother of all Victors,
Yangchenma, keeper of an ocean of melodies,
Jetsunma, compassionate liberator of beings,
Dakini of great kindness in Tibet,
Consort who pleases the enlightened mind of the
    Lotus-Born Vidyadhara,
Sole mother and only refuge of the people of Tibet,
Source of the profound secret Vajrayana teachings,
Conqueress of supreme knowledge, compassion,
    and power,
Vidyadhara accomplished in the supreme attainment
    of immortality,
Yogini who has perfected all the stages and paths,
Mother of skillful means, compassionately
    manifesting whatever form is necessary to
    subdue beings,
Goddess whose benefit for others is equal to the sky,
Ruler with naturally limitless, all-pervasive
    enlightened activity,
Jetsunma, if called upon, your compassion is swift.
If one is accomplishing you, you are a Dakini of
    most profound blessings,
Greatly kind one, whose compassion is like the love

of a mother watching over her children;
My sole protectress, who contains all objects
    of refuge,
Yeshe Tsogyal, to you I pray.
Queen of Dakinis, to you I pray.
The manifestation of power, to you I pray.
Radiant One of blue light, to you I pray.
Sole consort of the Lotus Guru, to you I pray.
Sole mother lineage holder, to you I pray.
Holder of profound treasures, to you I pray.
The one whose blessings enter quickly, to you I pray.
Glorious one who fulfills all wishes, to you I pray.
The one who accomplishes the hopes of beings,
    to you I pray.
Wish-fulfilling jewel, to you I pray
Deceitless compassionate one, to you I pray.
Constant protecter, to you I pray.
Dispeller of suffering, to you I pray.
Supreme guide of beings, to you I pray.
You are my Lama, you are my Yidam,
You are my Dakini, you are my Dharmapala.
Jetsunma, for an unfortunate being like me, you
    are my sole source of refuge.
I pray to you, with devotion from my heart.

By Ju Mipham. Translated by Dungse Thinley Norbu Rinpoche.
Excerpted from, A Cascading Waterfall of Nectar, pages 171–172.

A PRACTICE FOR THOSE WHO HAVE DIED

WORDS OF TRUTH TO ACCOMPLISH ASPIRATIONS

By the blessings of the Buddhas who have attained
the three kayas,
By the blessings of the unchanging true nature of reality,
By the blessings of the harmoniously united sangha,
May all the aspirations and dedication prayers
be accomplished!

The Mantra for the Accomplishment of all Aspirations

> TA DYA THA PAN TSA DRI YA
> A WA BO DHA NA YE SVA HA

(recite three times)

BRIEF SUKHAVATI PRAYER

E MA HO!
The wondrous Buddha of Infinite Light,
Amitabha. To his right is the Lord of Great
Compassion, Avalokiteshvara. To his left stands
the Bodhisattva of Great Power, Vajrapani.
They are surrounded by countless Buddhas and
Bodhisattvas. There is immeasurable happiness
and joy in the marvelous Pure Land called
Dewachen.

Instantly, when we pass from this life, without
taking another birth, may we be reborn in
Dewachen and see Amitabha's face.

Having made this aspiration prayer, may we
be blessed with unhindered accomplishment,
by all the Buddhas and Bodhisattvas of the ten
directions.

TA DYA THA PAN TSA DRI YA
A WA BO DHA NA YE SVA HA

(recite as many times a you are able)

Brief Sukhavati Prayer

(can be recited in English or Tibetan)

E MA HO

NGO TSAR SANG GYE NANG WA THA YE DANG

YE SU JO WO THUG JE CHEN PO DANG

YON DU SEM PA THU CHEN THOB NAM LA

SANG GYE JANG SEM PAG ME KHOR GI KOR

DE KYI NGO TSAR PAG TU ME PA YI

DE WA CHEN ZHE JA WAI ZHIN KAM DER

DAG NI DI NE TSE PHOE GYUR MA THAG

KYE WA ZHAN GYI BAR MA CHOE PA RU

DE RU KYE NE NANG THEI ZHÄL TONG SHOG

DI KE DAG GI MON LAM TAB PA YI

CHOG CHUI SANG GYE JANG SEM THAM CHE KYI

GEG ME DRUB PAR JIN GYI LAB TU SOL

TA DYA THA PAN TSA DRI YA
A WA BO DHA NA YE SVA HA

(recite as many times a you are able)

This prayer was given directly to Terton Migyur Dorje (1645-1667) by Amitabha Buddha in a vision.

Aspiration

May the truth of the Three Jewels,

The blessings of the Buddhas and Bodhisattvas,

The great power of the perfect completion of the
two accumulations,

And the power of the extremely pure and
unfathomable dharmadhatu enable us to fulfill
all the aspirations!

(recite one time at end of session)

THE ORAL TEACHINGS OF THE JOYFUL DHARMARAJAS
THE ASPIRATION OF SPREADING THE TEACHINGS OF THE EARLY TRANSLATION SCHOOL

At this present time even the wish to propagate the precious essence of the teachings through invoking the enlightened mind of the divine three roots possesses immeasurable merit. The purpose of this prayer is to completely perfect the aspirations of the descendants of the victorious one. By doing so one will encounter the yanas of the victorious dharma and its essence in all ones lives and then by holding, protecting and propagating these teachings, one will reach omniscience quickly. Therefore at auspicious times and in particular when the sangha gathers together, one should practice this aspiration.

NAMO

The sugatas and their descendants of the ten directions and especially the unequalled king of the Shakyas, the eight bodhisattvas and the hosts of noble sthaviras, the supreme embodiment of wisdom and love, please consider me.

The precious teachings that are the source of benefit and happiness, are presented by the supreme sage and bodhisattvas, but are again and again difficult to find and keep in mind.

May the teachings of victorious Padmasambhava flourish.

Shantarakshita, Padmasambhava, the dharmaraja
Trisong Detsen, the emanations of translators
and pandits, the yidam deities, the lineage of
vidyadharas of Kama and Terma, Ekajati,
Mahakala, Rahula, Vajrasadhu and the class of
wrathful protectors of the three tantras: mandala
of the three roots of the early translation school
please consider me. All the traditions of sutra
and mantra of the teachings of the Muni, were
brought through love to the Land of Snow.
Protectors, having considered your vajra samaya
to propagate them widely.

May the teachings of victorious Padmasambhava
flourish.

The vajra body, speech and mind of the
victorious ones of the ten directions, through
the miraculous play of the bodhisattvas of the
three families, cause the brilliant light of the sun
of benefit and happiness to shine in the Land of
Snow.

May the teachings of victorious Padmasambhava
flourish.

The great noble victorious one and his descendants
have assumed rebirth and emanation in accord
with their intention and have raised the victory
banner of the precious spotless teachings of the
Buddha.

May the teachings of victorious Padmasambhava
flourish.

The inherent power of all the common and
uncommon texts that have been translated,
corrected and established without error has
begun to open the great gate of illumination
in the Land of Snow.

May the teachings of victorious Padmasambhava
flourish.

The tradition of sutra and mantra for fortunate
disciples, is practiced with complete certainty
and so all the sutras and textual commentaries
are complete.

May the teachings of victorious Padmasambhava
flourish.

The great ocean of sutras that speak truth is
visibly beautified by the jewel of terma of the
profound dharma and thus the excellent path
of sutra and tantra are joined together.

May the teachings of victorious Padmasambhava
flourish.

The conduct of the wondrous abbot from
Zahore and the view of unequalled, excellent
Nagarjuna, are sealed in the Nyingma tradition
that unifies conduct and view.

May the teachings of victorious Padmasambhava
flourish.

Through the essence of the wisdom of the three
classes of profound inner tantra, the supreme
path of uncommon secret pith instructions, the
rainbow body blazes in wonder when passing
into the dharmakaya.

May the teachings of victorious Padmasambhava
flourish.

The eight principal sadhanas of the universal

peaceful and wrathful deities, and the essence of the wisdom of the individual transmission of the vidyadharas, are all gathered together and embraced as one in the tradition of Padmasambhava.

May the teachings of victorious Padmasambhava flourish.

The causal and fruitional vehicles of great Mahayana and Mantrayana, and the scriptures of the complete, unerring lineage of the vidyadharas, steam with the warm breath of the dakinis.

May the teachings of victorious Padmasambhava flourish.

The essence of amrita of the ultimate meaning of the teachings of Vajradhara, and the ear-whispered lineage spoken by millions of learned and accomplished ones, are not defiled by the fabrications made up by pretentious sophists.

May the teachings of victorious Padmasambhava flourish.

Even if one were to offer payment ornamented with gold and precious jewels, one would not receive the dharma of the heart treasure of the dakinis of space. This is only given with compassion to the fortunate followers of the teachings.

May the teachings of victorious Padmasambhava flourish.

The wisdom of the primordially pure essence arises radiantly as the spontaneously present nature. It is the great completion that transcends the mind of foolish meditation.

May the teachings of victorious Padmasambhava flourish.

By eliminating the reference points that cling to the individual aspects of existence and non-existence, and completely uprooting the mode of apprehension of extreme views, one realizes the unity of appearance and emptiness of ground, path and fruition.

May the teachings of victorious Padmasambhava flourish.

The ultimate meaning of the wisdom of the Buddhas of the three times, is unconditioned peace, simplicity and luminosity, the indestructible, vajra tenets of awareness-emptiness.

May the teachings of victorious Padmasambhava flourish.

The thick clouds of scriptures heard many times, blaze with garlands of thunderbolts of reasoning that subjugate opponents of the teachings as the rainfall of amrita of essential pith instructions fills one's heart.

May the teachings of victorious Padmasambhava flourish.

Through the path of wondrous secret Ati Yoga, the wisdom kaya of all the buddhas without exception is completely accomplished as the sovereign Vajra Manjushri.

May the teachings of victorious Padmasambhava flourish.

The roar of three kinds of correct valid cognition, strikes fear in the hosts of wild animals of the lower views. This is the melody of the lion, the supreme yana that pervades the three realms.

May the teachings of victorious Padmasambhava flourish.

The most excellent cloth of the completely perfect teachings of the Buddha, is topped with the beautiful finial of the essence of indestructible luminosity. This is the lofty victory banner victorious in all directions.

May the teachings of victorious Padmasambhava flourish.

May I and others, as long as there are sentient beings, preserve and propagate throughout the limits of space the completely perfect teachings and their essence.

May the teachings of victorious Padmasambhava flourish.

In brief, through the life examples of the learned, disciplined and accomplished ones, may the Buddha's teachings propagate throughout space. May the authentic holders of the teachings fill the earth.

May the teachings of victorious Padmasambhava flourish.

May the excellent guru's life be long. May benefactors of the teachings grow in wealth. May religion and society not decline and may the precious victory banner be raised high.

May the teachings of victorious Padmasambhava flourish.

The teaching taught by the immortal, lake-born, Buddha Padmasambhava possessing the splendid essence of all the victorious ones is known as the early translation school of the Nyingma. It is the grandmother of the victorious, perfectly complete teachings and has the distinctive quality of possessing a multitude of great essential profound teachings. It is the supreme excellent path of the joyful victorious ones and possesses completely pure view and meditation.

Having recognized this, one wipes this precious jewel clean and then places it at the top of the pole of the victory banner as an offering. For fortunate disciples it is the immensely powerful activity of teaching, debate and composition that when taken to heart spreads and flourishes in all directions.

Thinking in this way, these verses of auspicious aspiration have been set forth to accomplish the wishes of fortunate disciples.

From the heart, with completely pure excellent intention, Mipham Jamyang Namgyal Gyatso wrote down whatever came to mind in the morning session at an excellent and auspicious place and time. May virtue increase.

Sarva Mangalam.

The King Of Aspiration Prayers For The Excellent Conduct Of The Noble Ones

I pay homage to noble Manjushri Kumara.

To all the tathagathas without exception, those lions of men and women of the three times who abide in the countless worlds of the ten directions, I prostrate inspired by faith with body, speech and mind.

Through the power of this aspiration prayer for excellent conduct, I manifest in mind all the victorious ones. Bowing down with bodies as countless as atoms in all the realms, I fully prostrate to all the victorious ones.

I imagine on a single atom, buddhas as countless as atoms in the universe, each residing with his son and daughter bodhisattvas. In this way all the realms of the dharmadhatu are filled with victorious ones.

With oceans of inexhaustible exaltation consisting of all the sounds of oceans of various types of melodies, I fully express the qualities of all the victorious ones and praise all the sugatas. With the finest flowers, the finest garlands, music, perfumes, supreme parasols, supreme lamps and the finest incense, I make offering to all the victorious ones.

With the finest clothing, supreme scents, heaps of aromatic powders equal in size to Mount Meru and so on, all displayed in the most sublime of arrangements, I make offering to the victorious ones. Supreme victory banners and supreme pennants, all of these again I offer to the victorious ones.

Through the power of respectful faith in all the victorious ones, and through the power of trusting faith in excellent conduct, I prostrate and make offerings unsurpassable and vast to all the victorious ones.

Through the power of passion, aggression and ignorance, I have performed harmful actions with body, speech and likewise mind. All these actions I confess, each and every one.

I rejoice in all merits, those of the victorious

ones and their descendant bodhisattvas of the ten
directions, those of the pratyekabuddhas,
the shravakas requiring practice, the arhats who
no longer need practice, and those of all beings.

I request all the protectors, those beacons of the
worlds of the ten directions, who have traveled
the stages of the path of bodhi and have reached
enlightenment free from obscuration, to turn
the wheel of the unsurpassable dharma.

With palms joined, I supplicate all the tathagatas
who are planning to pass into nirvana, to remain
for as many kalpas as there are atoms in the
buddha realms, in order to provide benefit
and happiness to all sentient beings.

Whatever small virtue I have accumulated,
through prostration, offering and confession,
rejoicing, requesting to teach, and supplicating
to remain, I dedicate entirely for the sake of
enlightenment.

I make offering to the Buddhas of the past
and to those who reside in the worlds of the
ten directions.

May those who have not yet appeared as Buddhas,
quickly complete their intentions. May they
progress through the stages of enlightenment
and attain Buddhahood.

May the countless realms of the ten directions
be completely transformed into vast and
completely pure realms. May these pure realms
be completely filled with Buddhas together with
their son and daughter bodhisattvas, and may
each Buddha reside sitting under the greatest
of all trees, the tree of Bodhi.

May the countless sentient beings of the
ten directions be free from illness and enjoy
happiness at all times. May all beings who are
acting in accord with the goals of the dharma
be in harmony and may their aspirations be
accomplished.

May I perform enlightened activities and may
I recall all my previous lives. In all of my lives,
from birth to death, may I always be a renunciate.

Training by following the examples of all
the victorious ones, may I completely perfect

excellent conduct. May my activities and discipline be without stain and be completely pure. May my conduct at all times be free of faults and impairments.

May I teach the dharma in the language of the gods, in the language of the nagas, in the language of the yakshas, in the language of the Kumbhandas, in the different languages of humans, and in all the many languages spoken by sentient beings.

With a mind of peace, may I fully exert myself in the paramitas. May I never forget bodhichitta. May I completely purify without exception, all harmful actions and their ensuing obscurations to liberation.

May I be liberated from nonvirtuous actions, kleshas and Mara's activities that obstruct accomplishment, and may I act for all the beings of this world, just like the lotus unstained by mud and just like the beneficial sun and moon unhindered by space.

May I completely pacify the suffering of the

beings of the lower realms who in extent would fill all the directions of the Buddha fields. May I establish all beings in happiness and bring benefit to all.

May I completely perfect the activities of enlightenment and engage in harmonious activities in order to ripen sentient beings. May I fully teach excellent conduct and perform the sum of the above activities throughout all future kalpas.

May I always accompany those whose good actions are similar to mine. May our activities and aspirations of body, speech and mind be one and the same.

May I always meet those spiritual friends who wish to benefit me and fully teach me excellent conduct. May I never displease them.

At all times may I see in person the victorious ones, those lords who are encircled by their bodhisattvas. Throughout all future kalpas, may I tirelessly make a vast variety of offerings to them.

May I retain the authentic dharma of the
victorious ones and thus be able to shed
light on all enlightened conduct. Thoroughly
training in excellent conduct, may I practice
it at all times in all future kalpas.

In all my rebirths in samsara, may I obtain
inexhaustible merit and wisdom. In this way
may I become an inexhaustible treasury of
the qualities of upaya, prajna, samadhi and
liberation.

Within a single atom, may I see all the countless
Buddha realms. Within each of these realms may
I see the incomprehensible Buddhas residing
with their son and daughter bodhisattvas. As
they perform enlightened activities may I do
so along with them.

Then, in each of the realms in all directions, may
space even the size of a tip of a hair be filled with
realms the size of oceans containing oceans of
Buddhas of the three times. May I fully engage
in enlightened conduct together with the
Buddhas throughout oceans of kalpas.

Every single teaching of the Buddha appears in languages having oceans of qualities. It has the qualities of the pure melodic speech of all the victorious ones and harmoniously satisfies the different wishes of all sentient beings. May I always listen to the speech of the buddhas.

All the victorious tathagatas of the three times have fully turned the wheel of the dharma. May I, through the power of mind, fully enter into the inexhaustible melodious speech of all the victorious ones.

Just as the Buddhas enter into wisdom in all future kalpas may I too enter into such wisdom in this very instant. Combining the entire extent of all the kalpas of the three times into a fraction of a single instant, may I perform enlightened conduct wherever I may be.

In this very instant may I see all the lions of men and women, the tathagathas of the three times. May I at all times realize the liberation of the tathagathas that sees all objects of experience as illusion.

May I make the Buddha realms of the three times manifest within a single atom. May I then make each atom in all directions without exception manifest all the pure realms of the victorious ones.

May I go into the presence of all the present and future lords, those beacons who illuminate the world, who demonstrate stage by stage the attainment of enlightenment, who turn the wheel of the dharma, and who attain the ultimate complete peace of nirvana.

By way of the power of altogether swift miracles, the power of the vehicle that travels the path of complete benefit, the power of conduct having all excellent qualities, the power of all pervasive loving kindness, the power of all virtuous merit, the power of wisdom that is free from attachment, and the powers of prajna, upaya and samadhi, may I perfectly accomplish the power of enlightenment.

May I completely purify the power of karma, may I fully subjugate the power of the kleshas, may I render the power of the maras powerless,

and may I perfect the power of excellent
conduct.

May I completely purify oceans of realms,
completely liberate oceans of sentient beings,
fully see oceans of dharmas, fully realize
oceans of wisdom, perform oceans of excellent
activities completely purifying all faults, fully
complete oceans of aspirations, and fully offer to
oceans of Buddhas. May I perform all these
activities without weariness throughout
oceans of kalpas.

All the victorious ones of the three times
have made multitudes of enlightened aspirations.
May I become an enlightened Buddha through
performing excellent conduct thereby
completing all of their aspirations without
exception.

The principal son of all the victorious ones is
the individual named Samantabhadra. In order
to act in the same manner as this master, I fully
dedicate all my virtuous activity. I also make
dedication for pure body, speech and mind,
for pure conduct, and for the complete

purification of the realms. May I be just like
the master in making this excellent dedication.

In order to practice the excellent conduct of the
all virtuous dharmas, may my aspirations be the
same as those of Manjushri. In all future kalpas,
may I be without weariness in completing all
the activities of Manjushri.

May my paramita activities be immeasurable.
May my excellent qualities be immeasurable.
Having performed immeasurable activities,
may I attain all the manifestations of the
buddhas and bodhisattvas.

Just as space is without limit so too are all
sentient beings. Just as their karma and kleshas
are without limit, so, too, may my aspirations
be without limit.

An individual could offer limitless realms of the
ten directions ornamented with precious jewels
to the victorious ones. They could also offer
substances of gods and humans producing
supreme delight. They could make these
offerings in numbers as countless as atoms in the

realms over many kalpas. However, if they were to listen to this king of dedication prayers, be motivated to supreme enlightenment, and then give rise to faith even a single time, the merit gained would be even more sublime.

If I make this aspiration prayer for excellent conduct, I will abandon all rebirths in the lower realms. I will be free from associating with inappropriate friends and will quickly see the Buddha Amitabha.

I will completely obtain the supreme attainments, I will be happy in this life, and in this present life everything will go well.

In aspiring to be like Samantabhadra, I will be just like him in a short period of time.

If I perform the five inexpiable sins out of ignorance, when I recite this Prayer for Excellent Conduct, I will quickly and completely purify them.

I will attain wisdom, have a beautiful body, possess the major and minor marks, be born into an excellent family and be radiant in appearance.

The maras and tirthikas will not be able to harm me, and all beings of the three worlds will make offerings to me.

I will quickly go before the Bodhi tree, and abiding there I will be able to benefit sentient beings.

Having subdued the maras and their troops, I will attain enlightenment and fully turn the wheel of the dharma.

If I keep this Aspiration Prayer for Excellent Conduct with me, chant or read it, I will gain the complete fruition only known by the Buddhas, the attainment of supreme enlightenment —of this there is no doubt!

Just as Manjushri has supreme knowledge, so too, has Samantabhadra. In order to follow in the footsteps of these supreme bodhisattvas, I fully dedicate all the virtue arising from making this aspiration.

With dedications that are praised as supreme by all the victorious ones of the three times, I fully dedicate all of my roots of virtues in order that all beings attain the conduct of Samantabhadra.

At the time of my death, may all my obscurations be dispelled. Having seen Buddha Amitabha in person, may I instantly go to the pure realm of Sukhavati.

Having gone there, may all the fruitions of making this Aspiration Prayer fully manifest. May all of my wishes and those of others be completely fulfilled, and may I benefit sentient beings as long as worlds exist.

In that joyous realm having the excellent qualities of the mandala of victorious Amitabha, may I take birth on a beautiful lotus. May victorious Amitabha appear to me in person, and may I receive a prophecy from him.

Having fully received this prophecy in Sukhavati, may I emanate many billions of emanations, and through my intent, may a multitude of benefits be performed for sentient beings in the ten directions.

Through whatever small virtue I have accumulated by reciting this Aspiration Prayer for Excellent Conduct, may all the positive wishes of sentient beings and all positive results be accomplished instantly.

The merit obtained through the dedication of the Aspiration Prayer for Excellent Conduct is limitless and authentic. By whatever merit I have so obtained, may all sentient beings drowning in the river of suffering gain complete rebirth in the realm of Sukhavati.

Through this king of aspiration prayers may all sentient beings receive benefit and attain the greatest of all attainments.

By accomplishing this aspiration prayer taught by Samantabhadra that is ornamented with Buddha activity, may the lower realms be completely emptied of beings.

The Aspiration Prayer for the Excellent Conduct of the Noble Ones is complete. The Indian scholars Jinamitra, Surendra-bodhi, the translator Bande Yeshe De and others translated this text from Sanskrit into Tibetan and the great translator, Vairocana, served as the chief editor. Translated into English by Khenpo Gawang Rinpoche and Gerry Wiener. © 2012

THE THIRTY SEVEN PRACTICES OF A BODHISATTVA

NAMO LOKESHVARAYE

Although you see all phenomena without arising and cessation, you exert yourself solely for the purpose of sentient beings. To the supreme guru and lord Avalokiteshvara, I always respectfully prostrate with body, speech and mind.

The perfect Buddhas who are the source of benefit and happiness, arise from the accomplishment of the authentic dharma. Furthermore, that accomplishment depends on knowing how to practice. Thus, I will now explain the practice of a Bodhisattva.

1 At this time one has obtained the great ship of free and well-favored conditions difficult to find. In order to carry oneself and others across the ocean of samsara, day and night without distraction, to study, contemplate and meditate is the practice of a Bodhisattva.

2 Desire for family and relatives rushes like a river. Anger toward enemies blazes like fire.

The darkness of ignorance causes one to forget what to accept and reject. Abandoning one's fatherland is the practice of a Bodhisattva.

3 By abandoning disturbing places, one's kleshas gradually decrease. By being free from distraction, the practice of virtue naturally increases. Through clear awareness, one gives rise to certainty in the dharma. Abiding in solitude is the practice of a Bodhisattva.

4 Friends and relatives who have been together for a long time will part their separate ways. Wealth and possessions accumulated through effort will be left behind. The guest of consciousness will abandon the guesthouse of the body. Letting go of the concerns of this life is the practice of a Bodhisattva.

5 If one accompanies them the three poisons will increase, the activities of study, contemplation and meditation will deteriorate, and one will be separated from loving kindness and compassion. Abandoning bad friends is the practice of a Bodhisattva.

6 If you rely on them, one's bad faults will decrease, and one's excellent qualities will increase like the waxing moon. Cherishing spiritual friends as more precious than one's own body is the practice of a Bodhisattva.

7 Themselves bound in the prison of samsara, worldly deities – who can they protect? Thus going for refuge in the three jewels, the unerring protector of all, is the practice of a Bodhisattva.

8 The sufferings of the lower realms, extremely difficult to bear, are said by the Muni to be the result of evil deeds. Thus, even at the risk of losing one's life, never to perform evil deeds is the practice of a Bodhisattva.

9 The bliss of the three realms is like the dew on the tips of grass – in an instant it will disappear. Aspiring to attain the unchanging, supreme state of liberation is the practice of a Bodhisattva.

10 Our mothers have lovingly cared for us from time without beginning. If they are suffering, what is the use of one's own happiness?

Thus, giving rise to bodhichitta in order to liberate limitless sentient beings is the practice of a Bodhisattva.

11 All suffering without exception arises from desiring bliss for oneself, while the perfect Buddha arises from the mind of benefiting others. Thus, completely exchanging one's own happiness for the suffering of others is the practice of a Bodhisattva.

12 Even if others through great desire, were to take away directly or indirectly all my possessions, dedicating my life, enjoyments and virtues of the three times to them is the practice of a Bodhisattva.

13 Even if an individual were to cut off my head, though I had not paid them the slightest wrong, taking their evil deeds onto myself by means of great compassion is the practice of a Bodhisattva.

14 Even if an individual were to disgrace me throughout one billion world realms, giving rise to the mind of loving kindness and then proclaiming their good qualities is the practice of a Bodhisattva.

15 Even if an individual were to expose my hidden faults and castigate me in front of an assembly of many people, bowing down with respect with the perception of them as a spiritual friend is the practice of a Bodhisattva.

16 Even though a person that I nurtured lovingly as my own child, were to see me as an enemy, loving them even more just like a mother caring for a child struck by disease is the practice of a Bodhisattva.

17 Even though people equal to or below me in status, were to disparage me through pride, to respect them like a guru placing them at the top of my head is the practice of a Bodhisattva.

18 Even though I am poor, always disparaged by others, struck by severe illness and haunted by evil spirits, to be free from discouragement and take on the evil deeds and sufferings of all beings is the practice of a Bodhisattva.

19 Even though many people speak of me pleasantly and pay me the utmost respect, and even though I have obtained riches like those of Vaishravana, to see that the glory and riches of samsara have no essence and to be without pride is the practice of a Bodhisattva.

20 If I do not subdue the enemy of anger then the need to subdue outer enemies will only increase. Thus, taming one's mind by assembling the troops of loving kindness and compassion is the practice of a Bodhisattva.

21 The pleasures of the senses are similar to drinking salt water. The more you partake, the more your craving increases. Thus, to immediately abandon objects that give rise to attachment is the practice of a Bodhisattva.

22 All appearances are one's mind and mind itself is primordially free from the limitations of conceptual complexity. To understand the nature of mind and avoid giving rise to the characteristics of perceiver and perceived is the practice of a Bodhisattva.

23 When one encounters an object pleasing to mind, just like a rainbow in the summer time, to see it as lacking true existence even though appearing beautiful, and to abandon attachment is the practice of a Bodhisattva.

24 The varieties of suffering are like a child dying in a dream – grasping onto the true existence of such confused appearances makes one extremely weary. Thus, when encountering disagreeable circumstances, seeing them as confusion is the practice of a Bodhisattva.

25 If it is necessary to even give one's life away when desiring enlightenment, what need is there to speak of giving away external objects. Thus to give without expecting anything in return is the practice of a Bodhisattva.

26 If one cannot accomplish one's own benefit without discipline, it is laughable to think that one could accomplish the benefit of others. Thus, to guard one's discipline without yearning for samsara is the practice of a Bodhisattva.

27 To a bodhisattva who desires the riches of

virtue, all those who cause harm are like a precious treasure. Thus, to meditate on patience without resentment toward anyone at all is the practice of a Bodhisattva.

28 Even the Sravakas and Pratyekabuddhas accomplish their benefit alone, exerting themselves as if responding to their hair being on fire. Seeing that, to cultivate exertion, the source of qualities that benefits all beings, is the practice of a Bodhisattva.

29 Vipashyana that is fully endowed with shamatha completely subjugates the kleshas. Knowing that, to meditate, thoroughly transcending the four formless states, is the practice of a Bodhisattva.

30 If one employs the five paramita practices without prajna, one will be unable to attain perfect enlightenment. To meditate on prajna endowed with upaya, free from the concepts of the three spheres is the practice of a Bodhisattva.

31 If one does not analyze one's own confusion, one may act contrary to the teachings though appearing as a practitioner. Thus, to analyze one's confusion at all times and then to relinquish it is the practice of a Bodhisattva.

32 If, through the kleshas, one speaks of the faults of other Bodhisattvas, one's virtue will deteriorate. Thus, to avoid speaking of the faults of those who have entered the Mahayana is the practice of a Bodhisattva.

33 Through the power of honor and gain one engages in arguments one after another and the activities of study, contemplation and meditation deteriorate. Thus, to abandon attachment to the residences of friends, relatives and benefactors is the practice of a Bodhisattva.

34 Coarse language causes turmoil in other's minds and makes Bodhisattva activity decline. Thus, to abandon coarse language that is unpleasant to others is the practice of a Bodhisattva.

35 If one becomes accustomed to the kleshas, it will be difficult to apply an antidote to reverse them. Thus to hold the weapon of the antidote of mindfulness and attentiveness and to instantly subjugate the kleshas of passion and so forth when they first arise is the practice of a Bodhisattva.

36 In brief wherever you are and whatever you are doing you should examine the state of your mind. Possessing continuous mindfulness and attentiveness, to accomplish the benefit of others is the practice of a Bodhisattva.

37 The virtues that are accomplished through such exertion directed for the purpose of dispelling the suffering of limitless sentient beings, are dedicated to enlightenment by means of prajna that completely purifies the three spheres is the practice of a Bodhisattva.

Having followed the speech of authentic teachers, the meaning of the teachings from the sutras, tantras and their commentaries, are these thirty seven practices of a Bodhisattva. They have been composed for those who desire to study the Bodhisattva path.

Since I possess little intellect and small training, scholars may be unhappy with this composition. However, since this text relies on the teachings of the sutras and authentic teachers, I think it describes the unmistaken practice of the Bodhisattvas.

Still, the great activities of Bodhisattvas, are difficult to fathom by a person of lesser intellect like myself. Authentic teachers, please be patient with me and pardon any faults of contradictions, irrelevance and so forth.

Through the virtue that arises from this, may all beings, by means of supreme relative and absolute bodhichitta, be identical with the protector Avalokiteshvara who does not abide in the extremes of samsara and nirvana.

This was composed in the precious cave of Ngulchu by the monk Thogme, the expounder of scriptures and reasoning, in order to benefit myself and others.

I pray for the excellent health of the gurus,

I pray for their supreme long life as well,

I pray for the ever-increasing expansion of their enlightened activities,

Grant blessings to never be separate from the guru!

REQUEST FOR TEACHINGS

In accordance with the capabilities and the diverse wishes of sentient beings, I ask you to turn the dharma wheel of the common and uncomon yanas.

MEAL CHANTS

(Before Meals)

The unsurpassable teacher is the precious Buddha.
The unsurpassable protector is the precious Dharma.
The unsurpassable guide is the precious Sangha.
To these Three Jewels of Refuge, I make this offering.

(After Meals)

DEDICATION OF MERIT

By this merit may all attain omniscience.
May it defeat the enemy, wrong doing.
From the stormy waves of birth, old age,
sickness and death,
From the ocean of samsara, may I free all beings.

The Seven Fold Meaning of Choosing Pema Karpo (White Lotus) as the name of our center:

1. When Shakyamuni Buddha was born, it is told that he took seven steps. As he took each step a white lotus appeared behind him.

2. Padmasambhava (Guru Rinpoche), the great tantric master who truly brought Buddhism to Tibet, was said to have been born in the middle of a beautiful lake on a large white lotus. One of his names is Pema Jungney - the lotus born one.

3. The root teacher of Khenpo Gawang Rinpoche, His Holiness Pema Norbu Rinpoche's name means Jewel Lotus.

4. The white lotus is commonly used in teaching stories as the lotus grows in the mud and up through the mud but is not stained by it. Buddhas and Bodhisattvas take birth in samsara yet their nature remains purely awake. We are born into and believe in samsara but our indwelling Buddha nature is never stained by samsara.

5. Pema Karpo is dedicated to the dharma of awakening and we are located on the banks of the Muddy Mississippi River.

6. We use a Shakyamuni Buddha practice as the main sutrayana litergy for our center composed by Ju Mipham (1846-1912). The title of his extensive explanatory support is Pema Karpo.

7. For the Vajrayana we use the commentary by Ju Mipham on the Seven Line Supplication named Pema Karpo.

3921 Frayser-Raleigh Road, Memphis, TN 38128
901-377-4834 pemakarpomeditation@gmail.com
www.pemakarpo.org

Paintings by Guru Gyaltsen
GURUTHANGKA.COM

Made in the USA
Las Vegas, NV
27 February 2022